To my family for listening to every word
OVER and OVER and OVER again. Thank you.
And to the BIG, STRONG women in my life who
championed this book from near and far. Thank you.
—JC

For River and Summer—a mother's love
so strong it could light up the stars.
—JW

Text © 2024 by Jennifer Cooper
Illustrations © 2024 by Jen White
Cover and internal design © 2024 by Sourcebooks

This artwork was created in Procreate with a tablet,
digital pencil, and custom colored pencil and
gouache brushes.

Published by Sourcebooks eXplore,
an imprint of Sourcebooks Kids
P.O. Box 4410, Naperville, Illinois 60567-4410
(630) 961-3900
sourcebookskids.com

Cataloging-in-Publication Data is on file
with the Library of Congress.

Source of Production: 1010 Printing Asia Limited,
Kwun Tong, Hong Kong, China
Date of Production: April 2024
Run Number: 5032978

Printed and bound in China.
OGP 10 9 8 7 6 5 4 3 2 1

KATIE, BIG AND STRONG

THE TRUE STORY OF THE MIGHTY WOMAN WHO COULD LIFT ANYTHING

WORDS BY
JENNIFER COOPER

PICTURES BY
JEN WHITE

sourcebooks
eXplore

It was Saturday at the circus in Vienna many years ago.

A crowd had come to see Katie. They were all waiting to see just what she could lift.

Katie was **BIG**.   Katie was **STRONG**.

And...

KATIE COULD LIFT ANYTHING.

Katie Brumbach was exceptional.
She came from a **BIG** family with
fourteen **STRONG** children.
Legend has it that her mother's biceps
were each the size of
a holiday ham.

Her father could lift five hundred pounds with just one finger! Katie began performing with the family's circus act when she was just two years old. It was no surprise, because being strong was in her blood.

And when she felt **BIG** and **STRONG**, Katie felt like Katie.

But not everyone thought that a girl like Katie should be so BIG or STRONG or lift such heavy things.

"That's not the way," their voices would say.

"Girls should be slender."

"They're tiny and tender."

"Girls should never be BIG!"

BUT KATIE WAS.

And when challengers came her way, Katie did not back down.

ARE YOU STRONGER? TRY TO WIN

Many men lost matches against Katie. But one of them won
her heart when he proposed marriage.

He was a
sweet man
named Max.

And he loved Katie.
He loved that she was

BIG AND STRONG

and that she could lift him up way above the crowds to see the world...with just one hand!

Though the circus crowds in Europe grew and grew,
not everyone felt that a lady should behave like Katie.
"That's not the way," their voices would say.

"A lady is always quite weak!"

"She must be helpless and meek!"

"A lady cannot be that STRONG!"

SO KATIE LIFTED EVEN MORE!

She became strong enough to carry cannons on her back and lift full-grown horses without care.

Katie wanted everyone to know how strong she was. So, when a bodybuilder named Eugen Sandow was declared the "World's Strongest Man," she boldly decided to call herself...

SANDWINA

And then Katie Sandwina picked up her entire life with her husband Max and they boarded a ship to America.

In time, she became a star for the Barnum & Bailey Circus. And here, Katie took the center ring.

Katie wowed the crowds with her beauty and daunting strength. The wonder of Katie Sandwina was plastered on every street corner in New York City.

Katie was big, strong, and as successful as any man. But not everyone thought women should be equal to men. "Not today!" the statesmen would say.

"Ladies ought to keep quiet."

Katie felt it was time to be BIG and STRONG in a new way.
This time, she used her strength to lift women up in their cause for
suffrage—the right to vote.

Katie knew:

Women have voices.

Women need choices.

Women TOGETHER are STRONG!

Gathering at Madison Square Garden, the circus suffragettes rallied together for one thing: **EQUALITY**.

Even their mascot, a baby giraffe named Miss Suffrage, was up for the fight!

Eight years later, in the summer of 1920, women were given the right to vote in the United States of America.

And as time passed on, Katie continued to show off her muscles on the stage and at home.

Who else could raise a son to be a heavyweight boxing champ and then raise him above her head? Katie, of course!

When Katie finally stopped lifting husbands, horses, and hopes, it took many years before any woman could lift as much as Katie.

But that's not what really matters.

What matters is that Katie always knew that…

SHE WAS BIG, STRONG, AND BEAUTIFUL.

Because that's who Katie was.

About KATIE

Katie Sandwina was born Katharina Brumbach on May 6, 1884, in a circus wagon in Austria. Katie's family had a traveling circus act: Her parents and siblings performed feats of strength and acrobatics. By the time Katie was a young woman, she'd proven herself to be the strongest among her thirteen brothers and sisters. After every show her father would offer a cash prize to any person in the audience who could best Katie in a wrestling match. Legend has it that this is how Katie met her future husband, an acrobat named Max Heymann, when he stepped up to challenge her and she threw him to the ground! They married, established their own circus act, and made their way to America. Eventually the couple joined the Barnum & Bailey circus, where Katie became a star. Audiences were shocked and amazed to see Katie, clearly taller and stronger than Max, lifting him over her head with one hand and spinning him around.

In the early 1900s, Katie took the stage name "Katie Sandwina," naming herself after Eugen Sandow, a famous bodybuilder hailed as the strongest man in the world. According to a popular tale, Katie defeated Sandow in a weightlifting contest and took a feminine version of his name as a sort of trophy. While there's no evidence that such a contest ever took place, Katie had good reason to so boldly compare herself to Sandow: In 1911, she achieved the heaviest overhead lift ever performed by a woman—286 pounds, a world record that wouldn't be broken until 1987.

Throughout her career, Katie lifted, pulled, and supported all kinds of heavy things, including cannons, anvils, and a bridge that held the weight of several people at once. She could bend iron bars and break horseshoes with her bare hands, and in one of her acts, she used her strength to resist the pull of four horses. Many photographs show Katie holding two and even three people at a time—in one, she holds on one arm

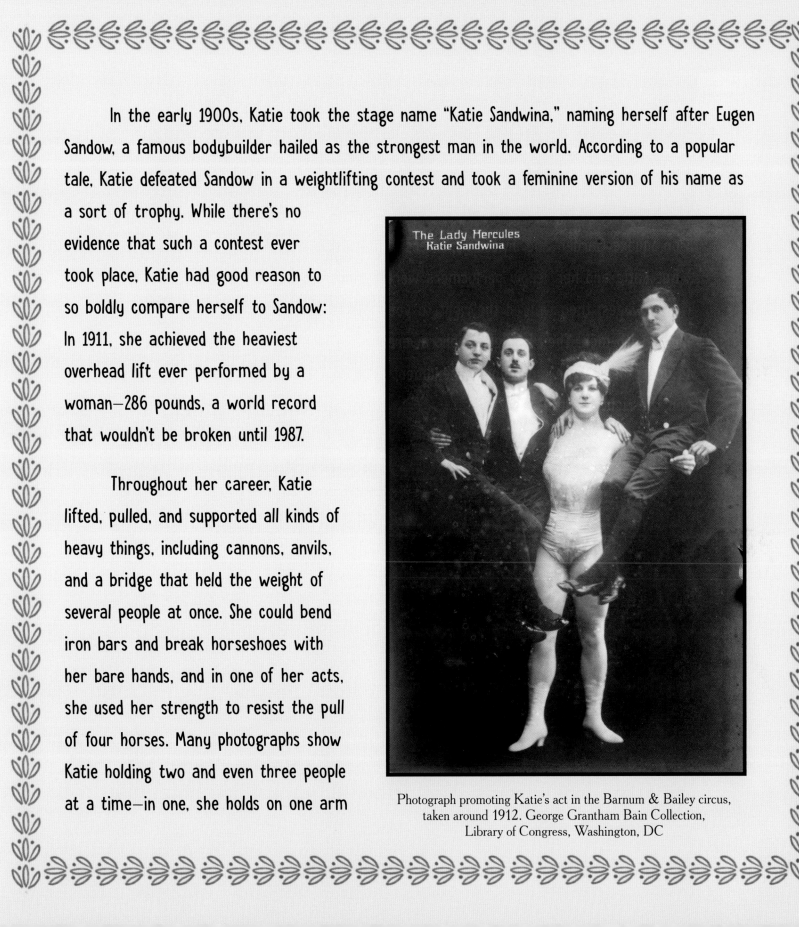

The Lady Hercules
Katie Sandwina

Photograph promoting Katie's act in the Barnum & Bailey circus, taken around 1912. George Grantham Bain Collection, Library of Congress, Washington, DC

Max, who in turn holds their firstborn son. (Years later, when this son became a heavyweight boxer, middle-aged Katie was still able to lift him with one hand.)

In 1912, at the height of her fame, Katie helped found the Barnum & Bailey's Circus Women Equal Rights Society. They held a women's suffrage rally in New York's Madison Square Garden and invited reporters, who mostly treated the event as a joke. But Katie and her fellow performers were serious—as women who earned their own wages, they wanted the right to vote and to be treated as equals with men. They brought public awareness to women's rights years before the Nineteenth Amendment granted women the right to vote in 1920.

When Katie retired from performing, she and Max opened a café in Queens, New York. Even in her sixties, Katie would sometimes demonstrate her strength to customers by breaking chains or lifting Max. She could also haul unruly patrons out the door!

Katie challenged the gender norms of her day by showing that being big and strong could also be considered beautiful. Generations later, she continues to inspire women athletes.

In 2017, the Arnold Pro Strongwoman contest was established as the world's most prestigious competition in women's strength training, and the winner receives the Katie Sandwina Trophy, a bronze statue of Katie.

Katie Sandwina was much more than just a strongwoman: She was a dedicated athlete, a caring mother and wife, a fearless suffragist, and a daring circus performer. Her legacy lives on through every girl and woman who knows that they, too, have a rightful place in the arenas of power and strength.

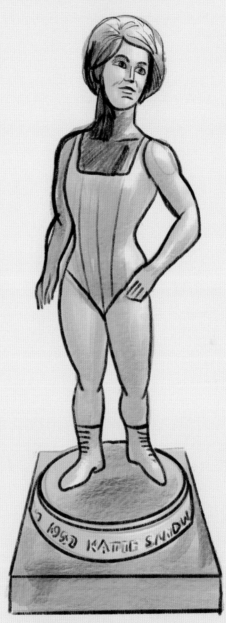

The Arnold Pro Strongwoman
Katie Sandwina Trophy